I Met a Guy…

and Other Things You Can Only Discuss with Your *SisterGirlfriends*

Valencia Joy

Write and Vibe Publishing

Cleveland

Copyright © 2020 by Valencia Joy

All rights reserved. No part of this publication may be reproduced, distributed, or transmitted in any form or by any means, including photocopying, recording, digital scanning, or other electronic or mechanical methods, without the prior written permission of the publisher, except in case of brief quotations embodied in critical reviews and certain other noncommercial uses permitted by copyright law. For permission requests, please address Write and Vibe.

This publication contains the opinions and ideas of its author. It is intended to provide helpful and informative material on the subjects addressed in the publication. It is sold with the understanding that the author and publisher are not engaged in rendering medical, health, or any other kind of personal or professional services in the book. The reader should consult his or her medical, health, or other competent professional before adopting any of the suggestions in this book or drawing inferences from it.

The author and publisher specifically disclaim all responsibility for any liability, loss, or risk, personal or otherwise, which is incurred as a consequence, directly or indirectly, of the use and application of any of the contents of this book.

Published 2020
Printed in the United States of America
ISBN: 978-1-953430-01-4 (pbk)
ISBN: 978-1-953430-02-1 (ebook)
Library of Congress Cataloging-in-Publication Data is available.

For information, address:
Write and Vibe Publishing
3675 Warrensville Center Road
P.O. Box 201372
Cleveland, OH 44120
cori@writeandvibe.com

This book is dedicated to all the SisterGirlfriends everywhere, who live by the code, lift their sisters up, love on them, and laugh with them often.

I would also like to thank my mother for always encouraging my writing.

To my two young kings, thank you for staying patient with me in all my endeavors.

And personally, thank you to my SisterGirlfriends who held me down throughout the years.

I love you all.

Introduction

I don't have any biological sisters. My only sibling is a younger brother. While having a little brother was fun, it also had its fair share of, "UGH," moments. I feel like I completely missed out on the feminine energy exchange that only sisters share.

All my life I have wanted sisters. I longed for them. There were times when I would watch *The Cosby Show* and become jealous of Sandra, Denise, Vanessa, and Rudy. I wanted someone to fight over clothes with and tease about boys and discuss pimple remedies.

I watched *Sister, Sister*, a sitcom about identical twin girls that weren't aware they were twins because they had been separated at birth! They found each other through happenstance and all of a sudden, lifelong friend. My envy showed while watching. They both had someone to yell, "Go Home Roger," with. I wanted sister unison.

It wasn't until I began to watch other shows like *Living Single*, *90210*, and *A Different World*, that I realized I could still have the sisterhoodship that I craved. Real sisters are nothing but girlfriends who become framily, you know…friends who have become family. And when I discovered the show *Girl-*

I Met a Guy...

friends, you couldn't tell me nothing! (I still watch *Girlfriends* and *Living Single* every night. It's a part of my self-care...we'll get into that later.)

The saying may be true for some, blood is thicker than mud, but when it comes to me and my SisterGirlfriends, blood couldn't make us closer, and I have a whole bunch. We're all different and that's a good thing. Can you imagine if we were all walking around wearing the same wig? It would be awful. We need the diversity! I don't know about you, but I feel like each group of SisterGirlfriends needs a variation of the following:

- The Dramatic One. She always says, "OMG!" to everything, big or small. You have a hang nail? "OMG!" Your car's gas tank is on empty? "OMG!" You never learned the wobble? "OMG!!" And she's always loud about it. The whole store, street, and anyone within a 10-mile radius can hear her, and think, "Dang! She's dramatic!"
- The Angry Dramatic. She's about to kill everybody. Kids acting up? She's 'bout to kill 'em! Boss getting on her nerves? She's 'bout to kill 'em! The dog barked? She's 'bout to kill 'em!
- The Mother. She's the comforting nurturer. Everyone goes to her for hugs or to be loved on. You don't want to disappoint her so you don't tell her some of the not so good stuff that you've done. If you ever heard her curse, you'd be shocked.
- The Over Communicator. She creates the group texts and the sub-group texts and the sub sub-group texts. She tells it all, not in a gossipy way, but in a y'all need to know, keep this between me and you, kinda way.

Valencia Joy

- The Practical One. She's more frugal than the rest. She would rather potluck than go out to eat. She coupons, so if she agrees to dinner out it's usually at a restaurant that she has a coupon for. And I bet she's never hurting for money!
- The Advisor. It's kind of like she knows everything but doesn't act like she does. She has a little wisdom, a little sage, a little life on her, and can get you to relax, relate, and release. Listen, everyone needs one of her. She is a life saver. She's calm and direct and loves but she's not the woo woo woo type. She doesn't like to go out a lot and she's not loud. But Lord have mercy if you've pushed her to anger, DUCK!
- The Been There Done That Know-It-All Advisor. It really doesn't matter what you are presently experiencing, she has already experienced it. You have a hernia? She had one two weeks ago. You wanna climb Mount Everest? She's already planning a trip. It may come across as her trying to one up everyone, but really, I think she just wants to belong and be relatable. I know I'm kind of giving her a pass with this one.
- The Party Girl. She is always the life of the party. Regardless the situation or circumstance, she will have a joke, get people laughing, and loosening up. She's probably the most blunt and outspoken. She's the one you have to alert that she's on speakerphone before she starts talking.
- The Social Media Guru. You know the one, always on social media, always going live, always taking pictures. She's her own brand. You can find her fighting in the comments on

celebrity posts. She's also a bit of a social media detective. She can see two sub posts and get to work, figuring out who the post was referring to by using high level intel to figure out when these two people last took a picture together and if they are still social media friends. She is also the one that will find out every bit of information her Sister-Girlfriend needs on a new guy.

I think I am good mixture of all these SisterGirl-friends.

And every group needs vocations. Doctors, lawyers, educators, resume writers, cooks, writers, comedians, and the like. I'd also like to point out the need for mechanics, a SisterGirlfriend that knows her way around a car. When I go to an auto shop, I feel like a silent alarm goes off, one that only the mechanics can hear. It screams, "Here comes money!" Like, they literally get a hard on. If I had someone to say, "Oh, a screw is loose on your muffler, that's what's causing the noise," I wouldn't have to put on the whole armor of God just to go get an estimate. Some women know how to take care of these kind of things; I am not one of them.

Which leads me to handy women. They know how to lay tile and hang pictures perfectly. Leaky faucets are not intimidating and sealant work is no match for her caulking gun. I proudly give the Rosie arm muscle flex to these women.

I personally know a ton of educators and counselors, which works in my favor when I have questions about my children's school, teachers, homework, or whatever else they need, because you know it's a lot.

Valencia Joy

My medicine friends come in handy, too. Just recently, I mentioned to my nurse friend that I had a painful stye forming on my eye. "Put a potato on it," she casually mentioned as she cut into her fried green tomatoes as we lunched. She paused slightly, then clarified, "Cut a potato and put in on your eye." As if I would have just put a white potato on my eye. Okay, I probably would have. This is why specifics are necessary in the medical field.

Then there are the financially savvy friends. They give advice on credit and stock markets, loans and so forth. You especially need a friend like this in your life to save you from spending your last dime on a supersized meal.

And let's not forget about the cooks, chefs, and bakers in your life that walk you through how to prepare certain meals. Not everyone was blessed to sit under big momma and 'nem and learn how to make cornbread dressing and macaroni and cheese.

I titled this, *I Met a Guy…and Other Things You Can Only Discuss with Your SisterGirlfriends*, because we all know that if you shoot a text like, "Hey sis, call me," depending on what she is in the middle of, determines the timeliness of her response and the response itself. You may get a phone call, you may get a, "Give me a minute" text, you may get complete silence because she is taking a nap, or getting waxed, or didn't hear the phone ding. And there is always that one annoying friend that doesn't even know where her phone is. She is in the top three most annoying friends ever. But if you text, "Hey, I met a guy," girl…they will all be ringing your doorbell within the next five minutes. They will help you analyze each excruciating detail from your meeting with said guy, what he meant when he held the door open for you, what he meant when he blinked, and what he meant when he asked, "Can I call you?" By the way, calling is totally different than texting or asking for your social media handle.

Meeting a guy is a pretty big deal. Talking it over with your SisterGirlfriends is an even bigger deal.

But before we go there, I need to tell you who you don't need in your circle, because there's good SisterGirlfriends and then there's the others. You don't need anyone around you who makes you feel stupid, all the time. Let's face it, we have all had ditzy moments where everyone looks at you and asks if you left your brain at home. I am not referring to that. I am talking about when she always has something to say about what you've said. She is negative toward your dreams, hopes, and ideas. She is an all-around naysayer and Negative Nancy. She's loud when you are losing, but silent when you win. When life has you hanging your head, she finds a way to knock your crown lower. She's not a friend, to you or herself. She needs to go heal. Listen, we have enough negative thoughts going on, we don't need our Sister-Girlfriends co-signing.

NOTHING GRABS YOUR SISTERGIRLFRIEND'S ATTENTION LIKE ANNOUNCING, "I MET A GUY"

Believe me. I know. There was a whole SisterGirlfriend summit the first time I made this announcement after my divorce. To this day, the summit still commences with each new guy. The questions are endless.

What does he do?
What does he bring to the table? Can he build a table? Does he put his feet on the table? Can he clean the table?
Has he been married?
How long has he been divorced?
How does he feel about divorce?
Does he have a 401K?
What do his teeth look like? Chicklets? Pearly whites or mother of pearl?
Does he have children?
How is his relationship with his baby mama? Does his baby mama know that it's over?

I Met a Guy...

Does he watch sports?
Does he watch the news?
Did he hold the door for you?
Is his mother still alive? How is their relationship?
Does he have sisters? You know they can be a trip.
Does he chew with his mouth open? Because you know how you are.
Will he activate your bad case of misophonia?
Does he snore?

You also must discuss the ins and outs of the meeting.
What did he say?
What was the inflection in his tone?
Body language?
Eye contact?
Where did you meet?
Was the sun shining or was there overcast?
Was it raining? If so, describe the rain. Was it a really wet, a drizzle, or a fine mist?
Was it snowing? The slushy kind? Or was there ice?
And in this current climate, does he social distance properly? Does he wear a mask? What kind of mask?
What color is the mask?

After all of the rigmarole, just like in Congress, there is a vote, or at least a final assessment to determine whether he is worthy to be dated, friended, or deleted. It's as if all your SisterGirlfriends sit around with auction cards, casting their vote. I wonder if guys actually know that their fate is in the hands of your SisterGirlfriends?

If he calls or texts during the assessment, all of the SisterGirlfriends are coaching you through your conversation and responses. And the convo is probably being had on speaker phone, unbeknownst to him. Poor guy.

Valencia Joy

I have a sis, who, with each new guy, our mantra to each other is, "Be Normal." It's a reminder to be yourself and to let things happen organically. I clearly do not follow this advice wholeheartedly because with each new guy I say, "I met a guy…will you be my bridesmaid?"

When I see a man wearing a suit or sweatpants, and he's smelling good with nice teeth, it's hard to "be normal." I'd like to pause here and pray that My Future Bae will fit this description. A good SisterGirlfriend would pray with me. Did you bow your head?

Men are handsome, but men like this are beautiful. I don't care how old you are, when a man that fits your style walks through a room, you pay attention. And you probably relay the experience to your SisterGirlfriends. So when he says hello, gets your number and calls within a reasonable timeframe, how can you not pick your bridesmaid dresses and the reception dinner? I'm usually prone to a jazz band for the reception party, myself. Funny enough, as I am making edits on this book, my SisterGirlfriend has text to say that she met a guy! They have been talking for a few hours so of course she asked if I can meet her at the bridal shop to try on dresses.

WHEN THE BRA COMES OFF, I AIN'T GOING BACK OUT

The freedom that comes with taking off your bra. Whether you wear an A cup or a Triple Z, every girl's girls breathe a huge sigh of relief when you let them escape that fabric prison. You can almost hear the sigh. And most of us have a simple understanding: "When the bra comes off, I ain't going back out!" I don't care what kind of emergency it is. Unless extreme death is involved (as opposed to normal death), we're going to stay put 'til the morning. Even then, it's a struggle.

    I used to be able to leave the house without a bra and no one would notice. Once I learned the "hide the nipple" hack, with Band-Aids or what have you, it was a done deal. (Yes, I used Band-Aids. I know there are fancy schmancy covers now. Judge not.) Those were the days.

    It wasn't until recently that gravity began to rear its jealous head. My boobs went from looking cute and perky in a tee to a little less cute and just being in a tee. I shouldn't complain too much. I'm thirty-nine and I nursed two kids so technically, I have retired boobs. I'm trying to convince myself that

Valencia Joy

a "slight natural sag" is still sexy…but anyway, back to the bras.

Underwire, padded, all bras suck. Every last one of them! And oh my goodness, the torture that is wearing the wrong size bra. Have you and your SisterGirlfriends decided that bras were invented by men that will never have to endure the uncomfortableness that they bring? My SisterGirlfriends and I have. Have you and SisterGirlfriends nodded your heads in solidarity when you think of the bold women that burned their bras? We have. Have you thought about doing the same? Not us! Bras cost too much. My one sis wears a Triple G and her bras cost the equivalent of a mortgage payment. They don't even come in pretty colors. She's stuck with black and white until some genius decides that big boobs deserve lacey red bras. Bras are an expensive rip off, like insurance. DO NOT EVEN GET ME STARTED ON INSURANCE!

Only a select few of us can roam the city streets without a bra. If you can, then you already know you are a member of the Itty-Bitty Titty Committee. If you don't belong to that committee then you're like me and are gravity's victim. May I tangent here for a moment? I was in the supermarket once with my sis. There was a woman behind us, possibly in her fifties, with a white t-shirt on and no bra. She didn't have half a boob to save her life, but her nipples were bigger than a little bit.

Not everyone can go bra-less. And the color of the shirt as well as the sagginess, or sitting prettyness of the boob, must be taken into consideration. SisterGirlfriends are good in this area. They can tell you when to grab the bra and when you have a few bra-less moments left!

Oh, the freedom that comes with going without undergarments. All of us have gone without panties at least once. Panty lines are gross. Can we agree? And while some of you cringe and "ew" at the thought, the reality is, most of us don't engage with panties, more often than not. At least this is my unfounded guesstimate. Maybe this changes with bigger booties. Do people with big booties wear underwear more? I don't know. There are some of us who wear shorts under everything, and those who think Spanx is underwear. (If you are wearing Spanx every day as underwear, please, please, tell me that you are washing them every night.) Admit it though, when you go without panties you feel a little sexier, a little naughtier, a little Eartha Kitt'ish in *Boomerang*. I can hear her now, "Marcus Darling...I don't have any panties on..." If you don't know the movie, go watch it.

   Foundation Pieces. That's what my mother calls a girdle, or Spanx. These days you can buy any variation of the generic, some of which will surprise you. I have legit had full-fledged conversations about the greatness of a pair of generic body shapers that I found at a dollar store. It's a testimony really, the way I tell it.

   You can always tell how great your body shapers are by how close you have to bend your knees together just to get in them and pull them up. When they are bent toward each other and touching, you are in for maximum suckage. That's a good thing. Or the degree to which it straightens your posture, when your back needs to stay straight when you are sitting, also a good thing. Or the indented lines that the garment leaves on your body when you take it off, that's a great thing.

   A SisterGirlfriend told me the same is true for control top pantyhose. I wouldn't know. I hate pantyhose. Detest them.

   My newest fascination is waist trainers. Have you used them? I've been using them for about two

Valencia Joy

weeks and I'm already down two notches! If Spanx is silver, waist trainers might be the gold. My posture is perfect; I'm sitting up completely straight. I have questions though. If I eat chicken wings and tacos while wearing them, does that cancel the waist trainer power? Anyway, when I've worn it for a month, I'll give a real review. But so far so good.

Every Woman Should Get to Slap Eve

Aunt Flow.
The horror that is menstrual cycles and cramps. I have a college friend who is kissing forty and she still calls it her "thing." I once went to the gynecologist, complaining about my aching ovaries. I pointed to my ovaries and he said, "So umm, that's not where your ovaries are." I would have laughed profusely but couldn't because my ovaries were aching too bad.

PMS. The insatiable need for chocolate and salty things. Bloating. Cramps. Irritableness. Crying at stuff you wouldn't usually cry over. Lord, have you ever had cramps in your back? I know I pretty much stand alone in this one, but my right ankle gives me the absolute blues EVERY MONTH! It's an ache deep in my ankle. I also get breakouts on my face. When I was in high school, I went home early one day every month because my cycle and my cramps made me puke. It was absolutely awful.

No one understands the horror of your period like your SisterGirlfriends. We've all had the conversation titled, "My Cycle is Coming," to which a good girlfriend will properly commiserate with, "Ugh…that sucks. Got your heating pad? Chocolate?

Valencia Joy

Good Movie?", and so forth. There is a survival kit checklist. Not for nothing, I totally think that we should get paid time off each month for periods.

And can we talk about when it comes unexpectedly? Or spotting? If you are a panty-less person, this can create a problem. Then, when you stand up and a gush of blood floods your panties. How dare it? I absolutely hate having to wear two pads, just for security. Has the stickiness from your pad ever stuck to your thigh, butt, or pubic hairs? (And if you have pubic hair, why aren't you waxing?!) It's a complete nuisance.

I could go on, and I will because you know what's the worst? Pulling out a dry tampon, after which your period re-debuts. We've all been there and if you haven't, I don't know if we can still be friends. Just for the record, pads feel like diapers and sound like diapers. They are diapers.

Listen, who invented sore nipples? Have your nipples ever been so sore that you can't even lay on your stomach? My first go-round of this was during my first pregnancy. Lord have mercy, that soreness was...sore! Now that my baby baking days seem to be behind me, I find that sometimes my nipples get sore right before my cycle. That alone, makes PMS rear its ugly head.

While we are discussing nipples, my Sister-Girlfriend is pregnant and was complaining of sore nipples. I made the comment, "You better toughen them up for nursing." I said it very matter-of-factly because I've been there. Twice. I probably also added a knowing head nod.

She asked a simple, inquisitive, teary, "How? I keep hearing that...how?"

Sis, I was stuck. Had not a clue. I also had been hearing it since my first pregnancy. It seems like sound, sage advice, especially since I know the pain of sore nipples while nursing a thirsty baby. Do you know how to toughen them up? I had NO CLUE. So, I looked her square in her eyeballs, which by the way, was filled with desperation and tears, and I said, "I don't know. Google it."

When your period doesn't come, for some, this is a joyous occasion. It means a baby is coming. It's a moment that you, your hubby, and your girlfriends have prayed for. This is where elation and tears of joy come in. A lot of clapping hands, giggles, and instant planning of nurseries and baby names begins.

I have had plenty of SisterGirlfriends share their preggo news and I have been so elated for them. The most recent was a text from a SisterGirlfriend who said she wasn't going to drink wine anymore. While texting back, "Why?", as that statement was a bit dramatic, she responded, "Well at least for the next 9 months," with a screenshot of her ultrasound. I was so excited for her! I squealed, "I knew it! I knew it!" while texting the same thing. Then comes the game of twenty-one questions, "What do you think you're having? When are you due? Are you hungry? Ew…y'all were doing it?"

For others, pregnancy comes as a shock to the whole system. I was young when I got pregnant, as in twenty-one years young. There is no word for nervous and scared but also extremely excited. My SisterGirlfriends were with me every step of the way. During the early weeks of pregnancy, when no one knew but me and them, my mother sent me to return a cable box (that'll give you a hint at how long ago that was) and my friend took the cable box out of my hand because I shouldn't have been carrying anything as a pregger.

I also remember walking into a church service, newly pregnant and definitely unwed. Being in church has a way of allowing you to reflect. I felt the weight of my decisions pulling my shoulders down. I felt the burden of everyone that I would disappoint. I felt the anxiety of not having the faintest clue of how to get through college, live life, or pretty much be someone's mother. I also felt the love brewing in my womb, a love I had never experienced before; my emotions were mixed. I stood in that sanctuary and cried. I boohoo'd. From the outside looking in, it probably looked like very bad acting in a church scene of a Tyler Perry movie. Three of my SisterGirl-friends were with me that day and they did not leave my side, nor did they judge me. When I felt like others were turning their backs on me, I could always count on them to stand shoulder to shoulder with me. We are still shoulder to shoulder to this day.

But either way, whether you are elated or shocked…only your SisterGirlfriends will understand. All of this, just from having a pair of ovaries.

I am a Christian, and I definitely believe in heaven and hell. While this is not in the Bible, I am pretty sure that Eve (and Adam) need to stand directly outside the pearly gates until the last soul has entered into eternity. Every woman should get to slap Eve and every man that has had to inadvertently deal with the effects of a cycle or pregnancy by way of his woman, sister, mother, auntie, cousin, or co-worker, should be able to gut punch Adam. This will be our final sinful act, and we will repent, then enter in. I have this all figured out in my head.

The Gynecologist.
As you read that you should hear scary music. I have sat in that flimsy gown, staring at those stirrups many a time, and I have snapped a picture to send in a group text. The response is the equivalent of texting, "I have a really bad cold," or "I ran out of bacon." Or

worse, "I ran out of wine." There is pity. There is sadness. Condolences are sent. "Aww, sis, I'm so sorry. What can I do? What do you need? Wanna grab dinner later?"

Once again, only a man could have come up with such an incredibly invasive and uncomfortable procedure that strips you of your last shred of self-respect. What I hate most, is the small talk that comes with it. The doctor is knee deep in my honey pot and asks, "So, read any good books lately?"

I'm all like, "What?"

I don't even want to participate in small talk when both my feet are placed firmly on the floor, my skirt is down, my panties (if I wore them) are up, and the doctor's hand isn't up my honey pot. So, imagine how much less of a conversationalist I become when I am in this mortified state. When that metal claw-like looking object opens me up I feel like the Grand Canyon I half expect tourists to walk by and take a picture.

Then comes the breast exam, while lying on my back. I've made no secret that I'm thirty-nine and my breasts don't stay up like they used to. They slightly fall to the side and then the doctor has to lift them back up to finish the examination. Afterwards, the doctor pushes on my stomach flab, making me feel extra squishy. Thanks doc. Thanks a lot.

What exactly are they feeling for when they do that? Did the doctor go to school and obtain a degree just to make me feel like a sloppy, fat version of the Grand Canyon? Lastly, what is the point of stepping out of the room while I put my clothes back on? At this point they have seen more of me than me and can tell me whatever they need to say while I put my panties on, one leg at a time, and my bra on, one boob at a time.

Valencia Joy

      I guess all this rigmarole is just preparation for having a baby because when those real contractions hit, all privacy is lost. Personally, I didn't care who saw me spread eagle on that birthing table, who so ever could help me get that baby out, come help!

Menopause.
I don't think I am there yet although I have announced that I do believe that I am in peripremenopause (pretty sure I made that up). I haven't gone to the doctor yet. And no, I haven't gone to WebMD either. You may be wondering how I can self-diagnose when I just told you I didn't fully know where my ovaries were. I understand. But trust me, I'm correct.
      I've listened to older woman discuss this. Remedies include ginger. One SisterGirlfriend bought ginger snaps, which turned into a whole discussion regarding if ginger cookies counted as a remedy for relief, while they sat around, eating said cookies and fanning.
      My other SisterGirlfriend's mother kept small fans stashed away or plugged in, in every room in the house. I saw them in the bathroom, the kitchen and in the front hallway. They were even on the couch, the kitchen table, and in between the house plants. She also had a small handheld fan that hung around her neck and a small one that she could plug into her phone. When I saw all of this, I knew menopause was serious business.
      I have always run hot and needed a lot of air. Sleeping with the window open all year round is my thing. I say that to say, I have experienced hot flashes since I was two. But these new age hot flashes are different. They hit me upside my head so hard that I can hardly see straight.

I Met a Guy...

I was once in Walmart, standing in line at the pharmacy when I struck up a conversation with the woman in front of me, as I am prone to do. Two minutes into the conversation, she took off her wig and started fanning herself because she was having a hot flash. Yep. You read that right. I felt so completely stuck and didn't know what to do. So, I stood there and held the conversation. On the inside I was cringing, "People can SEE US." But I could not abandon my SisterGirlfriend in her time of need. I couldn't let her stand there alone in her stocking cap with her wig in her hand while sweat poured down her face.

My prayer that night was, "Lord I pray that you remember what I just did there. And that if I ever flash that bad, that you send someone to stand in line with me."

While I am not looking forward to that stage in life, I'm glad I will have SisterGirlfriends to share it with.

I remember watching the Oprah Winfrey Show when she was diagnosed with premenopause. I thought she was being a smidge dramatic but now that I have night sweats, irregular cycles, horrible cycles, and random hairs on my chinny chin chin (I could totally compete with my 16-year-old son in the new beard department), I would like to amend my thoughts. She was not, in fact, being a smidge dramatic.

Auntie O, please accept my public apology. Lunch on me, okay?

Birth Control.
Some like it and some don't (much like the panty situation). It definitely has its pros and cons. While doing your research, as well as trial and error to determine what works best for your body, getting real life testimonials is important. Pills, IUDs, and the shot all

made me chubby. Honestly, it could've been the ice cream, but we will never know.

Let's pause for a minute because I feel like it's my duty to inform you that certain antibiotics are counterintuitive to the pill. I know this because I got pregnant with both of my children while on it. Imagine me rolling my eyes while simultaneously crying.

At some point I switched to an IUD and that didn't work so well either. I remember a time when it got stuck way up in my honey pot. I had to watch and endure in horror, and pain, while the gynecologist tried to get it out. She then had the nerve to ask if her med student could help?

Ma'am, I am not a guinea pig!

I posted on social media about my IUD getting stuck and was surprised at the number of women who replied saying they experienced something similar. It turned into an informative thread of chilling stories, all about birth control.

There are real side effects to birth control. Hair loss. Acne. Weight gain. Depression. Out of control hormones. Faulty tastebuds. Stroke. I almost would rather have another baby! Almost.

I am waiting for the day when the smarty pants scientists create birth control for men (other than vasectomies.) It's exhausting for women to always have to do all the work.

SEX AT 20 IS DIFFERENT THAN SEX AT 40

Sex.
When you had it. Was it good? Was it bad? Was it so bad that you had to go home and finish alone? All of these are topics of discussion at every age and stage of friendships because we all know sex at twenty is a lot different than sex at forty, or so I'm told. I haven't hit forty yet but from what other women have told me, chile I can't wait! I heard it was the bomb DOT com! I do have to confess that as I approach this glorious stage of life, my libido is revving. Lord, if you could just send the right man to test these theories, I'd be eternally grateful.

Depending on your age, marital status, or belief system, sex may not always be permissible and or accessible. So sometimes it comes with smidge of guilt. As your favorite SisterGirlfriend, if you're in this space and don't feel comfortable enough discussing sex, please skip this section. It's okay that you're uncomfortable, but know that other SisterGirlfriends are totally comfortable discussing sex. Neither side should be judged.

Valencia Joy

When a married sis complains about scheduling sex, or boring and routine sex, or having to have sex…as if it's a chore, the good single SisterGirlfriends let her know, the alternative can be lonely. If I'ma be honest…we discuss ad nauseam when sex becomes mundane and boring. Like, why is it bad? At what point did it get bad? What steps need to be taken to make it good?

And let's be honest, women can be way more graphic, detailed…and, well…nasty when it comes to their conversations. In my opinion, we can be way worse than guys.

For example, ever had a conversation about sweat and sex and positions? Detailed stories of what you like and what you don't like. Favorite places in the house to have sex. I know you have. This info comes in handy when visiting.

"Is this the couch where y'all tried that gymnastics move? Because if so, I'll sit somewhere else."

One of my SisterGirlfriends is adamant about not wasting her sex, as in it better be good. Like, she is very serious. It's a whole conversation. Another SisterGirlfriend has suggested that we should be able to take our sex back from encounters that aren't good. I like to call this, reclaiming my time! I'm all for it.

Then there is the conversation of sex that was so good, it made you cry. Like, literal tears. It'll have you quoting song lyrics and offering to cook. I particularly appreciate these conversations. I grab my popcorn and wine and say, "talk slow." And then there's the times when it's so disappointing, it makes you cry.

The intimacy that is included in sex. Making love. When your mental and physical connect and stars fly. That's the best. A beautiful connection. And as soon as you break away from him, you go tell your SisterGirlfriends.

Do you know your body? Do you know what you like? If not, you can't really get upset with a guy if you can't tell him what he needs to do differently.

Does size matter? Is this a touchy subject? I posted about this in one of my relationship posts on Facebook and the comments took me smooth out. While the men were beating their chests, bravo style, it was the women that schooled the readers. The conclusion was yes, size does matter, but also knowing how to navigate the motion in the ocean is just as important. Knowing where your g-spot is located is key and that's a whole other conversation. Just like a good selfie, it's all about the angles.

Toys.
If your SisterGirlfriend has found one that gets the job done and she doesn't sound the alarm in your friends group, she is not a good SisterGirlfriend. Kick her out.

I am in a women's self-care group and they understand that sharing is caring. Once we were in the middle of an orgasm challenge, and for the singles in the group, the conversation turned to testimonials of which toy to get. I didn't suggest any, but I did co-sign on one that was posted. I let them know it was good, but they needed to prepare for it. When asked how I responded, I said, "You gotta send the kids away, light some candles, prepare a romantic dinner, bubble bath, ask yourself how your day was…and make sure it's fully charged because the last thing you need is for it to die in the middle of the act."

SELL YOUR KIDS ON ETSY, NOT eBAY

Pregnancy.
Earlier, I touched on discovering you're pregnant. If you are pregnant and a little in your feelings, then skip this because we have to talk about some of the things that come with being pregnant. Crying at everything all the time. Loss of hair in the wrong places. I know a woman that lost some teeth. (It can happen.)

When I was about seven months pregnant it was Christmas time and I was trying to decorate when I casually mentioned to the wusband that I was hungry. He said, "Okay, what do you want to eat? I can go grab it."

I thought long and hard as I slowly untangled a string of Christmas lights. I pondered my options. What was around us? What would be open? What did my tastebuds want? Would my little muffin agree with my tastebuds? I said to him, "I don't know."

He then said, "Okay, well when you think of something, let me know and I'll go get it."

It was at this point that I became overwhelmed. I crumbled to the dining room floor and cried all over the floor and the string of lights. He looked at me like I had five heads. That only made me cry harder. He spoke slow and deliberate, enunciating everything, "Uh, did you hear me say that I will go and get it for you?"

I got upset, trying to explain that it is very upsetting to be hungry and not know what you want to eat. Needless to say, it was a rough night. I think that string of lights is still sitting on that floor. I have since moved.

Bladder control becomes an issue. To this day, every time I sneeze, I get a little fearful. And Lord don't let me laugh a little too hard.

I had insomnia so bad that I started watching television until television finally started watching me. It became a nightly ritual that, I am ashamed to say, I still follow, all these years later. I have started to ween myself off it, but I am not 100% yet.

I was told that if you had heartburn during your pregnancy, then your baby would have a head full of hair. Well, during my first pregnancy, while I dealt with insomnia, I also dealt with heartburn. So much so that I slept sitting up, until gravity took a hold and drug me down to a sleeping position. Then, heartburn would wake me up and I would have to sit up again. All. Nine. Months. My son was born with so much hair it was unreal. I was not impressed.

Eventually the waddle comes. Everything in the nether regions spread to a point where walking regular just isn't an option. Let me tell you, by months seven, eight, and nine, the few seconds during walking where all your weight shifts to the right side of the waddle, the left side is thankful. And when the weight shifts to the left, the right side breathes a sigh of relief.

And the clothes. Now, they are cute, but when I was pregnant I had a meltdown in a maternity store because nothing was fashionable. Nothing. I

Valencia Joy

yelled at the store clerk as if she were in charge of purchasing. (Let's pause for an apology. Dear Store Clerk, if you're reading this, I do apologize. I was growing a human inside my body. That's my excuse.) One time, I walked in Victoria's Secret and asked this jerk of a clerk if they had a maternity section. She laughed and said, "Maybe online," which made me cry.

I started the mommy journey by myself. While I was pushing out baby number one, the rest of my SisterGirlfriends were receiving college diplomas. So, I had to do trial and error without the luxury of picking up the phone and crying and commiserating with anyone. However, most of them are mommies now and I love listening to the tales.

One of my favorite memes right now on being a mother is where one mom texts another, "I'm done!! I'm selling my kid on eBay!"
The other mom responds, "Don't be silly! You made him!! Sell him on Etsy!"
Absolutely hilarious and so true. Who else would understand hard conversations with your kid? When they are young, they ask you to describe God. When they get a little older, they want you to describe sex.

#gulp

There are so many things that go along with parenting. Can you identify a croup cough? Jaundice? Do you let them cry it out or do you hold them often? Do you breastfeed? Which diapers should you purchase? Where can you find tips and support on how to parent a special needs child? When is it time to potty train? When and how do you teach them to drive? Do you teach abstinence or hand them condoms? How do you teach them to show respect while keeping their spunk and voice? Should you make baby food or buy it? How do you deal with attitudes and sassiness?

I Met a Guy...

      This list does not do the parenting questions justice. When you feel overwhelmed with no help, SisterGirlfriends to the rescue. Not for nothing, raising teens needs its own support group.
      Also, just so you know, I didn't get my college diploma with my SisterGirlfriends, but I did get it later. High five me!

Miscarriages.
It's devastating. I almost didn't want to touch on this because it's so intimate, and everyone deals with this type of grief differently. But this is one of the times you need your SisterGirlfriends the most. Even if you have your hubby or baby's father or your mom, you still need your sisters.
      I have sat with a few SisterGirlfriends when they have miscarried, and I've experienced my own. There are really no words to describe the feeling. Empty? Lost? Hurt? It's hard to make sense of it, no matter how hard we may try. Here are the only two things I feel pressed to say.

1. If you go through this, please don't do it alone. I pray you have a great support system that includes SisterGirlfriends, but they can only be there if you allow them. What I've noticed is that some women shut down to a dangerous level. They don't talk, they don't share, they don't let people in. That's not healthy. You need to be able to let it out and express your pain. You need to find a safe space to heal. You can't do that if every ache and question stay internal.
2. SisterGirlfriends, just be there. Grief is complicated and intricate enough without you adding to it. While people mean well, a lot of their words end up hurting more. It's best to just be quiet. I would imagine this isn't exclu-

sive to miscarriage, but any loss or death or grief. Just keep your mouth closed unless you truly feel led to speak. She will remember your casseroles. You cleaning the house. You taking the kids for the day. In those most intimate SisterGirlfriends moments, when you comb her hair, or hug her until she breathes, or when you're simply sitting with her in her grief…she will remember that most.

HEY GIRL, DON'T JUMP OFF THE CLIFF

Mommy/Daughter Arguments.
    These kinds of arguments hurt, especially since for most of us, we can't even argue like we want to. You can't tell your mama she's wrong. Or to shut up. At least my friends and I can't. If you can, girl, you need a different kind of book. But seriously, have you talked to your friends about an argument you had with your mom?
    SisterGirlfriends give a different perspective and whether they agree or disagree, they will remind you that she's still your mama and that you only get one. In extreme cases, your SisterGirlfriends can encourage a course of action. And when they see your mama, they will still greet her with, "Hey Ms. So and So," with a hug and smile.

Daddy-Daughter Issues.
I have them (insert cry face) but I had no idea how many other people have them. The more you talk about them out loud, the more you realize a lot of your life and love decisions are based on these issues. I never would've guessed that my wusband was a lot like my father until I started speaking on my father's

characteristics. One of my SisterGirlfriends said, "Sounds like someone else I know," and I immediately went, "WHOA!"

Therapists and counselors are good for this kind of issue as well, but a good powwow with your SisterGirlfriends can also be therapeutic.

After becoming an adult and having children, a failed marriage and so forth, I remind myself to look at my parents as humans. They weren't these perfect beings who knew everything. They were imperfect human beings that did the best with what they had, and the best with what they knew to do. Seeing them in this light makes a huge difference.

Watch Your Step.
I have watched men shake their head after seeing their friend skip off the cliff. There is no warning, no anything. A man once said to me, "Men don't really give each other advice because he gotta learn the hard way, like me."

I was dumbfounded. They really think like that. Male relationships with each other are weird and I don't get it. They watch their best friend make some of the dumbest, most horrific decisions that could've been avoided and yet, they don't say a mumbling word. They are just available for a beer afterward like, "Hey, I know you broke your whole body flying off that cliff, but can I buy you a beer?"

Seriously?

I reposted something like this in one of my relationship posts on social media, and to be fair, most every man that responded was mortified that women think this type of behavior exists. Most expressed that while they do have serious conversations that include accountability with each other, they just don't broadcast it for others to hear. They were insistent upon the fact that true friends do hold each other accountable and have intimate conversations that never leave the circle. I hope this sentiment is true.

Listen, if I am ever about to make a dumb decision, I want people that I KNOW love me, to pull me to the side and say, "Listen here SisterGirlfriend, up ahead is a cliff and I see you speeding towards it. Turn right!"

Advice from your SisterGirlfriends is important.

Therapy.
I love a good powwow with my SisterGirlfriends, but sometimes we have issues that the group can't talk through. I think in previous generations, therapy was as taboo a thing in conversation as money and sex were. Thank God, things have changed. I am such an advocate with checking in with someone. It's okay for those check-ins to be weekly, monthly, yearly, however often you need it.

Although I know how to pray, how to laugh, and how to hug, sometimes a professional is needed. I will never judge a woman for acknowledging that she needs help or for taking the steps to get it. I have sat on many a couch, crying "fix me" to some poor unsuspecting counselor and I still go from time to time. Truthfully, I have an upcoming appointment.

Life is complex and therapy helps as much as you let it. Meaning, therapy requires honesty and transparency on your part. You have to be your truest self in that hour or so in order to become your better self. This is not the time to fake it 'till you make it, but more to allow your rawest self to appear. The space is safe, and the result is a better you. Being able to share with your SisterGirlfriends about what you're learning in therapy, about yourself, about life, coping skills, etcetera, is important. It helps you to stay accountable to your growth.

Valencia Joy

Self-Care.
I often ask my SisterGirlfriends how they self-care. It's one of my standard questions when I interview women on HeyVeeTv (make sure you check it out on YouTube). Self-care is fairly new...taboo even. I don't think women are used to intentionally doing things that solely bring them some type of enjoyment and peace. It feels selfish to take a long bath when you know there is laundry to be done.

I understand how it feels to get your nails done when you know the dishes need to be washed, or to take an extra thirty minutes to journal when you know lunches need to be made. I get it. But it needs to be said that if you constantly pour into everyone else, as most women do, without ever pouring into yourself, you will be miserable. And because we tend to the thermostat in our homes and surroundings, everyone else will be miserable as well.

You need a space and an activity for you. I tell my SisterGirlfriends to rest their capes, take a break, and figure out that thing that will make them feel recharged. Then, do that thing.

I know it may be hard to figure out what makes you happy. Women are so used to pouring into and supplying for others, that we are grossly neglected. Why do we think it's okay to neglect ourselves?

Find your self-care routine and share your discovery with your SisterGirlfriends. The world won't end if you self-care. In fact, the world will be better if you self-care. Or at least, your world will be.

Faith.

I Met a Guy...

I am a follower of Christ and my faith is very important to me. Very. But if I am being honest, sometimes, it wanes. I know the Bible says all we need is faith the size of a mustard seed (we love to quote that) but there are moments when something that small doesn't seem attainable. Here is where your SisterGirlfriends come in and I know this personally. I know what it means to have big faith in a big God and petition for my SisterGirlfriends. I don't care what they are going through, I stand tall with "God can, and God will." However, when it comes to me and my petitions to God, I am much less bold. Just like I stand in the gap for my SisterGirlfriends, sometimes I need them to stand in the gap for me.

  It's good to trade our stories about how life started tripping but God made a way. What an encouragement, for your own prognosis, listening to what God has done in another SisterGirlfriend's life. Even better than talking about what God did, is dishing on WHO God is. Discussing His love, grace, and forgiveness. Finding new revelations about Him in scripture. Discovering new layers of His love. Remembering that God provides.

  It's all a beautiful walk. All this and more, you need to hear from your SisterGirlfriends, and they need to hear it from you.

My Wusband Cheated
and it was the
Highlight of Our Marriage

Cheating.
When you think he's cheating, that's one thing, but when you catch him cheating…LORD! This is devastation. It's another topic that I almost don't want to touch, but here goes. I have plenty of experience with this. When I caught my wusband cheating it was definitely the highlight of our marriage. Each new indiscretion revealed another new one and my head was reeling. It became a rabbit hole of new information; the length of his affairs was mind blowing. One affair was half the duration of our marriage (that's seven years).

While there are women out there who are grimy, lack self-respect, and are downright ugly-…knowingly sleeping with married men, there are other women who are the standard for Girl Code, what is right, and honoring each other. If you ever have to deal with infidelity in your marriage, I pray that your tribe has women who will hold you down while you heal. My tribe cried with me, prayed with me, and sat with me.

I Met a Guy...

As if the whole process wasn't humiliating enough, I had to sit on a hospital table and ask for every STD test possible. It was absolute torture because my family doctor knew that I was married and eventually had come to know that we were not the only two in our marriage. My SisterGirlfriends gave me the courage to go and get tested, get counseling, and heal.

They also stopped me from calling other women, busting windows, and slashing tires. I can laugh now, but back then I lost my laughter amongst all that turmoil.

Basic Arguments in Marriage.
He leaves the toilet seat up. He leaves the toothpaste on the counter. He doesn't communicate like I need him to. He doesn't come to bed when I go to bed. He wants the thermostat on sixty degrees, I prefer seventy-five. The biggest one of all: does the toilet tissue go over or under?

We all know these complaints well, whether from our own situation or from listening to our married SisterGirlfriends. Listen, many times these complaints are annoying but not argument worthy. Talk-it-out worthy? Yes, but not argument worthy.

Sometimes it's healthy to have a powwow about him, without him around, with your SisterGirlfriends. It's like, when people suggest writing out your issues and then burning them. Think of it as a symbolic gesture that helps you feel better. Sometimes sharing your angst over something that is, let's face it, trivial, helps you feel better. It gives you enough energy to endure another round of the toilet tissue sitting on top of the toilet tissue holder while the holder still holds an empty roll. Let's take a moment of silence while you woosah.

Valencia Joy

One of the greatest pieces of relationship advice I heard came from the movie, *Insecure*. "Do you want to be right or do you want to be in relationship?"

As long as that relationship is still serving you, choose your relationship (within balance).

Divorce.
I have a little bit of experience in this area. HA! Listen, divorce is like a death. Death by force, is what I called it when I was deep in the throes of the philosophy of it all. It is awful. It hurts like you wouldn't believe. You find yourself thinking about all the good times, or trying to remember a good time. All the bad times that should've served as red flags but didn't. Or maybe they did but you ignored them. The hard decision to actually leave. How it affects the kids? The family? You? The devastation and heartbreak if he leaves. And everyone has an opinion. All of a sudden, divorce is all you see on television and hear on the radio. It's like you're drowning in it. The lawyer is constantly in your ear.

I remember waiting for a court appointment and my wusband's attorney sat next to me. He purposely tried to bully and antagonize me with the fact that my wusband's mistress was pregnant. Then he tried to "advice" me to death. They were all failed manipulation attempts because that day, I laced him with my Black Girl Magic!

During the process, your emotions are all over the place. One day you're sad and depressed, the next day you're angry and lonely. The silence in my home when my kids were with my wusband was so deafening it almost burst my ear drums.

Your money pivots but your bills don't. I remember having to learn how to prepare dinner for

I Met a Guy...

three instead of four (because I don't like leftovers). I still don't have that down pat but it's all good.

The first time you reach for your wedding ring and your finger is bare, you're startled. You feel really single in a world full of doubles.

It's all so much. If you are going through this, I am here, as your newest SisterGirlfriend, to tell you that it will be okay, and you will be just fine. I know that you may not feel like it and things may not look like it. Believe me I know. But I promise, one day your smile will return, your laughter will have weight, and your joy will balloon. There is life after divorce. My prayer is that I'm just reiterating what you've already heard from your other SisterGirlfriends.

My SisterGirlfriends sat with me as I dealt with the weight of divorce as well. I am pretty sure that I would not have been able to survive had it not been for my faith and my SisterGirlfriends.

Woman Up and Wail to Jesus

Working Out.
Ever been on the phone with your SisterGirlfriend and said, "Oh my God, I am getting so fat," all while you eat ice cream from the carton, or a whole plate of cookies? This always leads to standing up and not being able to see your toes. And you're not pregnant.

    I have a SisterGirlfriend who is my prayer partner. Every morning we text our specific prayers for the day, then attempt to pray at the top of every hour. Her recent text to me was, "discipline to work out." I put my phone down.

    One time my bestie had me to join a bootcamp. Looking back, this was her way of saying I was getting a little chunky. So, we paid our hard-earned money to join said bootcamp. With this, we got a set number of exercise classes per day and a meal plan.

    The instructor happened to be obsessed with Whitney Houston so that's all we worked out to. In order for the songs to fit our workouts she increased the tempo so a lot of it sounded like Alvin and Chipmunks were singing instead. Have you ever heard Alvin belt out, *I Will Always Love You*? It isn't quite

I Met a Guy...

as moving as Whitney but still, I did okay with the exercises.

It was the meal plan that went bad. I was literally preparing two different meals, one for my family and something bland and small for me. Theirs looked so much better and I found myself nibbling on their food. That turned into making a small plate of their food for myself after I had eaten my own. That turned into sitting down to their dinner, then still making a smaller plate later, plus my own plate.

Then came weigh in day. I had my whole plan ready. I was going to say that I was on my cycle and the weight gain was because of that. What I did not know was that weigh in was in front of everybody. I started to get nervous. When it was my turn, I said my lines as rehearsed, only quietly, "I started my cycle, I think that's what may have caused the weight gain."

I actually thought I would be looked at as admirable, because I had pushed through and still came to work out, despite living through my monthly curse. The instructor kept acting like she couldn't hear me. She then said loudly, "I don't understand how it could be that much of a gain!"

She checked my BMI and that had gone up too. "No, something else is going on, for your BMI to go up as well!" She looked at me pointedly.

I'm laughing as I tell y'all this but know that I was beyond humiliated. She kept talking loudly in disbelief. I don't quite remember how this exchange ended but I can tell you, that was my last class. Bestie was disappointed in me. On the upside though, she lost weight.

Brazilian Waxes.
Oh. My. If you like them (the process, not the after effect) you may be a bit sadistic. My very first wax

story I probably will never fully write about. It was that horrific. Humorous as all get out, but horrendous. Let's just say I only got it half done. After the esthetician had done the "front" she instructed me to get on all fours. I was still getting my hearing back from the searing pain that was "doing the front" so I was confused. "All fours for what?"

"So I can do the back?"

"The back of what?" I countered.

"The butt," she replied.

"No ma'am," I yelled. "Ain't no way I'ma let you do that again, this time on my butt! You shoulda got the toota when you got the roota!"

I proudly walked out of there with a mullet. Since then, I've woman'ed up and completed the mission, but not without some sweat and wailing to Jesus.

Others have lied to me, including my wax lady, and said that with each visit it gets easier. It does not, my friend. There is great anxiety filled anticipation when you know she's about to let 'er rip. And just like at the gynecologist office, when you are on your back for your yearly visit, and someone is knee deep in your honey pot (we talked about that earlier), they try to have meaningless conversations with you. Because if you sit in silence, it can become awkward. You're alone with your thoughts-your inner you-and your inner you just might tell you to jump off that bed and run out, panty-less.

If you've never been waxed, it goes like this:

Esthetician lathers on the hot wax. "So, read any good books lately?" Rips the wax off, and also rips away your soul. You yell.

Lathers on hot wax. "Politics, right?" Rips the wax off and rips away your soul again. You yell.

I Met a Guy...

Lathers on the hot wax. "Think the Cavs are gonna pull it off this year?" Rips the wax off and once again, rips away your soul. You yell.
"Hasn't this weather been so crazy?"
Afterwards you lay in the fetal position and rethink your whole life.
"See you in six weeks?"
You say, "Yes. Thank you."
Only your SisterGirlfriends understand this level of crazy torture, that you readily pay for. Every. Six. Weeks. The payoff is great though. You feel all super sexy and silky.

Beauty by Numbers.

Manicures and pedicures are important but so is the price. Who does the best eyebrows, hair, nails, and wax? It's good to know who does the best work but won't break the bank. You also need to know whose work is worth breaking the bank for.

It ain't nothing worse than jacked up eyebrows. Well, there is one thing worse. When you and your SisterGirlfriend's eyebrows equally slay but you paid ten dollars more, a discussion needs to be had.

Speaking of worth, when is Old Navy having a sale on jeans for the whole family? When is Bath and Body Works gonna put the 3-wick candles on sale? When is Victoria's Secret having their six panties for twenty-five dollars sale?

Now, online boutiques are competing for my dollar. Fashion Nova, Fenty (the lingerie and the make-up), and lest we forget, the mother of all online shopping: Amazon.

Knowing these deals helps me budget for my hair. I have had about every hairstyle known to woman and that includes the Jheri Curl. Blame my mom for this. I was in elementary school and she made all the decisions.

Valencia Joy

I've had bad weaves, wigs, color, cuts, and so forth. I'm sure because my style is a bit eccentric, no one truly knew if it was just a part of my "look" or if it was a mistake. Either way, there was always one SisterGirlfriend that said, "Uh, Vee, no." Even if my pride was bruised or my feelings were hurt, I was thankful for her candor.

Shoes.
Need I say more? Buying a new pair of shoes is almost like bringing home a new baby; it's such a joyous occasion. Everyone claps and oohs and ahh. Your SisterGirlfriends don't necessarily need to talk shoe sales. Just shoes. Period. High ones. Flat ones. Sandals. Boots. Sneakers. Wedges. Shoes.
What an orgasm.

REALITY TV SHOW DATING IS A BIG DEAL

Pop Culture/Reality Television.
Who's dating who in pop culture? Who is falling out and who is getting together? Who got married and how were the wedding pictures? Who fought and who is moving on? This is all a very big deal.

There is nothing like talking about these folks with your SisterGirlfriend as if you actually know these people in real life. Through reality TV you get a bird's eye view of it all and it is so entertaining. In fact, my SisterGirlfriend just text me last night about the recent episode of *Iyanla, Fix My Life*.

"Uh uh, because I really think he loves her."

I like to think of myself as an investigator of some sort, so when I figure something out before the news actually drops, I take a bow. Through this, I learned if TMZ hasn't verified it then it may be fake news.

As you can see, television is my guilty pleasure. I watch the ratchet and the respectable. I can talk *Housewives* (I'm currently weening myself off this show), *Chrisley's, Braxtons, Masked Singer* and so forth. After a long day, short day, or just a day, I love to turn on the TV and see what's going on. My latest obsession are the social experiments that are dating shows. *Love is Blind* captivated my heart and I have also fallen in love with *Married at First Sight*. Once my children are grown, if I am still single, I am definitely going to apply.

I also love scripted shows and dramas. *Greenleaf, Queen Sugar. Insecure. This is Us*. Again, I speak about these characters with my SisterGirlfriends like I know them personally. We guess what was going through their minds during the show, as if they shared that information with us. To me, that's a good sign of excellent writers. It keeps us talking like we are part of the family.

I'm also a sucker for the corny Christmas movies on Hallmark and Lifetime. It gives me hope that when I pass through a small town and my car breaks down, that the man who stops to help is not only the small-town sheriff, but also the mayor, and is in charge of the annual Christmas dance and bake-off. And that's where we fall in love and kiss under mistletoe. Oh, he's also the real Santa clause. Hey. It can happen!

I'm not being a couch potato though, so there is no need to be worried. None of my Sister-Girlfriends would allow me to slum. Watching television is a part of my job, as I just wrapped a web series with my writing partner in crime. Be on the lookout for Live Love and Lies the web series!

Friends Wipe Your Tears and Your Snot

Singing and Dancing.
Okay, maybe this is just me and my SisterGirlfriends, but to this day, if we hear a certain song, or phrase, it's on. Listen, we could be across the room and it's as if we both heard the invisible whistle. We search for each other, lock eyes, and then, queue the performance.

Girl's Night Out.
Isn't it fun to dress up? To wear a sexy dress, put on cute heels, makeup, a good wig, and go out. Many times, we make plans with the best of intentions, anticipating the fun, then, when the time comes, we aren't quite as excited. Maybe that comes with age. I don't know. It takes a bit of effort to work a full shift, come home, get your kids, family or pets together, shower and then change. (Remember when we talked about how if you take off your bra there isn't a really good chance you're gonna put it back on?) But then the texts start rolling in, asking all the questions to get you excited again. What're you wearing? What time are you leaving? Wanna ride together? Before you

know it, excitement sets in and you're ready to go. A girl's night out is always worth it.

The conversations over drinks and appetizers is usually just what the doctor ordered. Ahh, what I wouldn't give to talk about politics, love, likes, marriage, dating, come to Jesus moments, engage in some venting sessions and indulge in some genuine laughter like, right now.

Girl's Night In.
As much fun as girl's nights out are, there is immense entertainment in partaking in girl's nights in. As I'm writing this, I am reflecting on this one girl's night in. It was potluck style at a SisterGirlfriend's house. We curled up on couches, ate pizza out of the boxes, burned candles, and listened to music. With some girl's nights in you just need that soothing atmosphere. With others, you just need to laugh until you cry and cry until you laugh. Whether in or out, it's always magical when SisterGirlfriends gather. It's uplifting and free.

Finances.
Sometimes you gotta tell your SisterGirlfriends just how broke you are. Not everyone is a financial guru. Not everyone can budget. But all can be taught. I used to sit in front of an Excel spreadsheet and go from tears to confusion and back to tears. All those tiny little blocks and my personal disdain for numbers threw me all out of whack. I'd end up saying "it'll just hafta work itself out," and walk away.

It wasn't until one of my SisterGirlfriends took a look at my finances, what I was bringing and what I was putting out, and filled all those little boxes with the appropriate numbers and got me straight!

I Met a Guy...

Prayer Partners.
Sometimes it feels like it's hard to get a prayer through. Maybe devastation is too heavy, or depression is too heavy, or you just don't know the words to pray. Hey sis, listen, I've been there. There is nothing like being able to reach out to a SisterGirlfriend and have her go to God on your behalf. It's an honor to be able to talk to God for my SisterGirlfriends, to war against the bad with the ultimate weapon, God. It's even better when we can corporately come together and pray, praise, and petition God. I will never take that lightly.

Tears...and Snot.
I will never forget when I was at my friends' wedding. What should have been a super joyous time was otherwise tainted by my wusband's affair. So, as my friends were saying "I Do" and kissing and being all romantic and stuff, I was swallowing a lump in my throat, trying to figure out where my life had gone wrong. I excused myself to the bathroom, where I had planned to wipe a tear or two, then return to the festivities. But as I looked at myself in the mirror and saw how pitiful I was, I sank into a chair in front of the vanity, laid my head on the counter and wept. Like, ugly cry wept.

With no energy to heave or to breathe or to wipe the tears, I barely lifted my head and saw three of my SisterGirlfriends reflections staring back at me in the mirror. Without much discussion, and absolutely no knowledge of what had upset me, one grabbed the tissue and wiped my tears and my snot. That moment was profound for me.

A Place of Refuge.
When I got divorced and my kids left home to spend time with their dad, my house instantly got quiet. Too

quiet at times. All of a sudden, no one was wrestling or karate chopping the air. There were no thumps that made me yell, "What was that?" There were no starving quests for food, as if they didn't eat twenty minutes ago. There were no video games. No music playing. No playful hugs.

There was complete silence and I could not handle it. So, I called a SisterGirlfriend. I spent more time on one or another of my SisterGirlfriend's couches. They kept me laughing, handed me tissue when I cried, and snacked with me. Another Sister-Girlfriend let me spend the night at her house often. In the morning, I would get up and move my car to let her hubby out, then come back inside, maybe eat breakfast, maybe mope, maybe write, maybe watch TV. Eventually she told me it was time to get back to life. Refuge.

Standing Up for Yourself at Work.
Do you remember that commercial where the girl was rehearsing her request for a raise in the bathroom? She kept stopping and starting, trying to get her words and phrases just right, not knowing that anyone could hear her. Then, a toilet flushed and a SisterGirlfriend came out of the stall to wash her hands. Before the SisterGirlfriend left, she turned and said, "Go for it."

There ain't a thing wrong with rehearsing with your SisterGirlfriends. They can offer unique perspectives and encouragement. We all need that "go for it" cheer.

There is also a time to talk about those raises and bonuses. It's hard enough garnering respect in the business world but when your hard work is paid off with more money…well, let's celebrate.

This type of encouragement is important because most fields are male driven. Many times it

I Met a Guy...

seems like we, as women, have to really work the balancing act to defend ourselves or our positions without giving off the impression that we are a witch, on our period, or too sensitive. It sucks, right?

Someone to Gas You Up!
Sometimes you need life to be spoken into you. You need a SisterGirlfriend to remind you just how dope you really are. To remind you of all the things that you offer when life would have you think otherwise. And you need them to speak loudly in order to drown out any other voice that may speak contrary. You go girl!! They have to remind you of exactly who the cuss word you are! These moments usually leave you feeling invincible.

Online Dating.
I hate it. Detest it. It feels like...like a bad reality show. You put all your details and a few pictures out there and wait for Mister Right and all you end up getting is Mister Huh? As I type this, I see the irony in the fact that I don't like online dating but am anxious to be a contestant on a show. Oh well.

Anyway, as you decide whether to swipe left, right, up or down, diagonal, or log out, you need your SisterGirlfriends. First, you need them to quell the anxiety that swells as you go on a new site. You need them to cheer you on, tell you how her friend at work found the love of her life on this site, to tell you to stop being a punk and go ahead and plug in your information, all while she complains because she has to go have sex with her husband. It makes you wonder why you're so anxious to get married.

After all this, you get off the phone with her and find a single SisterGirlfriend to commiserate with. You tell her about this site and talk her into joining. Your most influential line is the fact that your

Valencia Joy

other SisterGirlfriend's friend at work has had success and found the love of her life. Then you both hop onto the online dating site, fill out the required information, choose profile pics together (that's the most important part-to get your profiles just right), and count to three before pressing send.

And nothing!

But then, the most "I would not date him" type of man inboxes you and then someone worse than him comes along. It's a mess.

A male friend once told me I needed to sift through the duds. SIFT?! Listen, I don't thrift shop because I don't want to SIFT. I don't have the patience unless someone goes with me and holds my hand and sifts for me. Online dating is like thrift shopping. If you've had success, then God bless you.

I have not. I am still waiting to have that serious moment when I text my SisterGirlfriends,

"I Met a Guy…"

Hey Sis

As you can see, I take my SisterGirlfriendships very seriously.

I do realize that there are levels and categories to this though. Some are closer than others. Some, you've had longer than others, while some are better at some subjects than others. And that's okay.

Not every SisterGirlfriend is going to be your bestie, nor should you hold every SisterGirlfriend at arm's length. I used to be the biggest advocate for inclusion (I sometimes still struggle with this). I used to think everybody deserved every part of me, and everyone should be included in all of my plans and every aspect of my life. Now I know that's not the case. Instead, everyone has a section. Everyone that SHOULD have a space, fits somewhere. However, the standards and requirements to be a SisterGirlfriend in my life are pretty much the same: respect, love, honesty and laughter. You get bonus points if you can cook!

My prayer for every sis that comes across this book is that she has a tribe of SisterGirlfriends. A tribe of women who love you through the hard times, are your prayer partners, secret keepers, reminders of God's promises, giggle buddies and more. Women that clap hard for you, tell you when you're wrong, and wipe your nose when you cry.

It's hard to be a woman. Although we were chosen for this life and built for the road, that doesn't mean it's easy. A reminder that you've got what it takes, goes a long way. And knowing you've got women walking with you, gives you strength.

If you've ever spent more than thirty seconds with me, you know my heart is geared towards healthy relationship and friendships. A healthy you needs healthy SisterGirlfriendships and vice versa. I've built a good portion of my life's work on building up and encouraging women. HeySis, a women's empowerment organization that I founded, is where broken women come to heal, and healed women help. It's girl talk for women and you can check it out at www.HeySis.org.

I also co-wrote, produced, and directed a web series centered around the SisterGirlfriendship of five women dealing with life and love. You can check out *Live Love and Lives* on YouTube.

Relationships are important. SisterGirlfriends are more important! So, do me a favor and share this book with your tribe. Giggle and share and agree and disagree. When you're done, email me at valenciajoy.fowler@gmail.com and let me know what y'all have deduced.

Cheers to you!

Your favorite SisterGirlfriend,
Valencia Joy

About Vibes: We are a hybrid publishing company that believes writers should only have to worry about writing. Meaning, you write your book, we'll do the rest.

To learn more about us, our authors, and their books, please visit us at

Writeandvibe.com | Fb & IG @writeandvibe

www.ingramcontent.com/pod-product-compliance
Lightning Source LLC
Chambersburg PA
CBHW021431070526
44577CB00001B/165